Biological Secretions Aid in Resolving Felony

LET'S UNCOVER THE CRIME

ALIZA BANO

Printed and bounded in India.

Dedicated to my parents

Zakir Ali and Nahid Bano

Contents

Preface

Forensic science is a crucial field that plays a vital role in solving criminal investigations and providing justice. Over the years, advancements in various scientific disciplines have greatly contributed to the development of forensic techniques. In recent times, the study of biological secretions has emerged as an invaluable tool in forensic science, aiding investigators in unraveling the mysteries surrounding crime scenes. This dissertation report aims to provide a comprehensive understanding of the role of biological secretions in forensic science. It emphasizes the importance of utilizing these secretions effectively to enhance investigative techniques and improve the overall efficiency of forensic analysis. By exploring the various biological secretions and their forensic implications, this report aims to contribute to the advancement of forensic science and its application in solving criminal cases.

The prologue of this book provides a base of introduction to forensic science, emphasizing the role it plays in criminal investigations and the challenges faced by investigators. It highlights the need for innovative techniques and the potential of biological secretions as a valuable source of evidence. By examining the historical context and key milestones, we have gained a deeper understanding of how forensic science has transformed into a crucial component of the criminal justice system. The review of forensic science development has revealed that the field has progressed from simple observation and deduction to a multidisciplinary approach that integrates various scientific disciplines such as chemistry, biology, physics, and psychology. This interdisciplinary collaboration has greatly enhanced the accuracy, reliability, and objectivity of forensic analysis.

The epilogue of this book focuses on semen, saliva & sweat as a biological secretion and its significance in forensic science. It explores the components of saliva, including DNA, enzymes, and other proteins, and their forensic implications. The chapter discusses the use of saliva in identifying suspects, determining time of death, and assessing drug and alcohol presence. Biological secretions left at crime scenes are valuable sources of evidence. Through DNA analysis, fingerprinting, saliva and bite mark examination, semen analysis, blood analysis, and sweat and odor analysis, investigators can extract vital information that helps in identifying, connecting, and prosecuting criminals. Biological secretions provide crucial leads and contribute significantly to solving crimes and ensuring justice.

Aliza Bano

FOUNDATION of FORENSICS

Prologue

In the modern era, crime rate is increasing day by day because of a lack of education, money problem, psychological factor, etc. In dwindling the crime rate Forensic Science plays a vital role.

Sir Arthur Canon Doyle made Forensic Science famous by his fictional character Sherlock Holmes.
Also known as Father of Forensic Science.

Forensic Science is science used for the purpose of law and helps in the resolution of legal disputes. It refers to the application of scientific knowledge to legal problems, especially scientific analysis of shreds of evidence scavenged from the scene of crime & which is a critical element in the criminal justice system. Every piece of evidence has its own scientific value. To sum up, in a line, Forensic Science is a branch of science that solves Crime.

1.1 Forensic Science

The word Forensic comes from the Latin word Forensis, meaning "open court" or "public". In legal terminologies, it is a sort of science that deals with the principles and practices of different branches Forensic science relies on the use of various tools and techniques, such as DNA analysis, fingerprinting, ballistics testing, and computer forensics. It also involves the use of expert testimony in court cases to help explain complex scientific evidence to judges and juries. Overall, forensic science is a critical component of the criminal justice system, helping to solve crimes and bring justice to victims and their families.

STANDARD DEFINITION- Forensic Science comprises a detailed examination of evidence recovered from a crime scene after investigating it properly which helps to punish the culprit frenetic.

RELATED LAW- The Indian Evidence Act (IEA), originally passed in India by the Imperial Legislative Council in 1872, during the British Raj, contains a set of rules and allied issues governing the admissibility of evidence in the Indian courts of law.

- Sec 3 of IEA, defines evidence, including:

  - All such statements that the court allows or needs to be presented before it by the witnesses in connection to matters of fact under inquiry. These statements are termed as oral evidence.

  - All such documents including any electronic record, presented before the court for inspection. These documents are termed documentary evidence.

- Sec 45 of IEA deals with the opinion of people who are called experts, including:

- There are matters mentioned in the section in which help is required from witnesses having experience and skill and the opinion given by such witness is expert opinion.

- The court cannot form a correct judgement without the help of a person with special skills or experience in a particular subject. When the court needs an opinion in a subject which requires special assistance, the court calls an expert, an especially skilled person. The opinion given by a third person is considered as relevant facts if the person testifying is an expert.

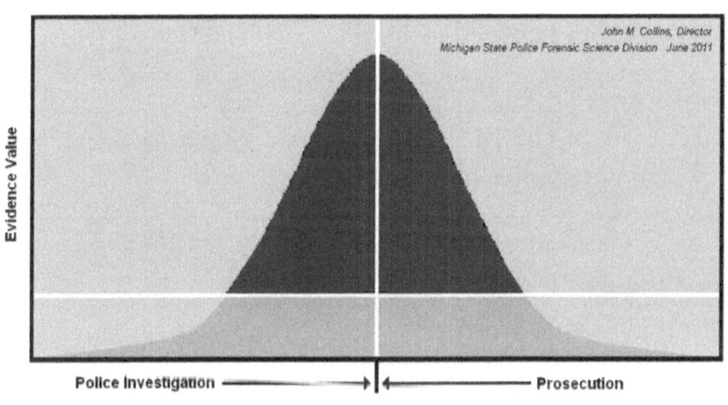

Chart: Forensic Science Impact Curve

1.2 History of Forensic Science

Forensic science has been around for quite some time; however, it was not originally recognized by the law enforcement community as a means of solving crimes. Its origins are owed to those first individuals that developed and fine-tuned the principles needed to identify and compare physical evidence Forensic science has been around for quite some time; however, it was not originally recognized by the law enforcement community as a means of solving crimes. Its origins are owed to those first individuals that developed and fine-tuned the principles needed to identify and compare physical evidence. Evidence of forensic science being used to solve a crime goes all the way back to 44 B.C. and is tied to the death of Julius Caesar. Some of the better-known are listed here along with their discoveries:

• Mathieu Orfila (1787 – 1853) considered to be the father of forensic toxicology
• Alphonse Bertillion (18953 – 1914) devised first system of personal identification
• Francis Galton (1822 – 1911) development of fingerprinting and classification
• Leone Lattes (1887 – 1954) discovered blood grouping
• Calvin Goddard (1891 – 1955) ballistics comparisons
• Albert O. Osborn (1858 – 1946) document examination
• Walter C. McCrone (1916 – 2002) analytical technology
• Hans Gross (1847 – 1915) application of scientific disciplines
• Edmond Locard (1877 - 1966) Locard's Exchange Principle

Table: History of Forensicb Science

1.3 Development in Forensic Science

Modern techniques involving very sophisticated machines and procedures help forensic scientists solve crimes. Technology has speeded up and improved analysis and data retrieval, making possible the ability to store vast amounts of information about criminals – information that can be readily exchanged within and between law enforcement agencies. This timeline is a comprehensive listing of all the significant events in the development of forensics. However, many of the significant events have been listed here to show the progression of scientific sophistication:

A book titled as Ming Yuen Shih Lu mention the use of fingerprint in 6th century (China)

Forensic Science Timeline	
Year	**Achievement**
700s	Chinese used fingerprints to establish identity of documents andclay sculptures, but without any formal classification system.
ca.1000	Bloody palm prints were meant to frame a blind man of hismother's murder.
1149	Idea of having a coroner was started by King Richard of England.

1248	A Chinese book contains a description of how to distinguish drowning from strangulation. This was the first recorded application of medical knowledge to the solution of crime.
1910	First comprehensive hair study.
1920	Weapon manufacture data is categorized
1920s	Tool mark comparison used.
1921	First polygraph (lie detector) developed
1924	First U.S. police crime laboratory.
1932	FBI established (Forensic Bureau Investigation)
1941	Voice print identification technique developed.
1954	Breath analyzer for field sobriety testing developed.
1957	Skeletal growth stages the basis of Forensic Anthropologyidentification
1960	First laser design used to identify fingerprints.
1967	Tests for dried bloodstains developed.
1971	Photo-fit enabling witnesses to piece together facial features developed.

1980	Method developed for detecting DNA differences.
1983	First use of personal computers in U.S. police control cars provide quick information from National Crime Information Centre.
1984	Genetic profiling using DNA developed.
1987	First time DNA evidence used to get a conviction in the U.S.
1991	Automated imaging system developed to compare marks left onfired bullets
1996	FBI introduces computerized searches of a fingerprint database.

Table: Forensic Science Timeline

1.4 Principles of Forensic Science

Forensic Science consists of all the branches of science and their applications in the justice system. Originally, all the techniques were borrowed from various discipline like chemistry, medicine, surgery, biology, photography, and mathematics. The principle of all natural sciences is the bases of Forensic Science. Broadly, there are 7 basic principles described below:

- Principle of Individuality
- Principle of Exchange

- Principle of Progressive change
- Principle of Comparison
- Principle of Analysis
- Principle of Probability
- Principle of Circumstantial facts

1- Principle of Individuality: Every object natural or man–made is individual in character, that cannot be duplicate. The law of individuality is fundamental in forensic science. Anything that is involved in the crime scene is unique. Thus, the culprit is unique, his weapon of offence is unique, scene of crime, evidentiary clues, leftover and picked up by the culprit are unique. We only must identify the uniqueness to link the crime with the criminal.

2- Principle of Exchange: The French scientist Edmond Locard formulated "Whenever two identities come in contact, mutual exchange of traces take place". The law of exchange is also known as Locard's principle of exchange. Thus, Edmond Locard is known as "Father of modern Forensic Science." When a criminal or his weapon of crime meets the victim or the objects surrounding him, thus the mutual exchange of traces takes place between the criminal, victim and the object involved in the crime.

3- Principle of Progressive change: Everything changes with the passage of time. Nothing is permanent and immutable. The rate of change varies with different objects and under different situations. The scene of occurrence undergoes rapid changes. The objects of the crime scene, the weather, the human beings, undergoes changes in a comparatively short period of time.

4- Principle of Comparison: Only the likes can be compared with the likes. It emphasizes that the necessity of providing corresponding samples/specimens for comparison with the questioned samples/specimens.

5- Principle of Analysis: Anything can be analyzed. The principle clarifies the necessity of correct sampling and correct techniques for useful and worthwhile results.

6- Principle of Probability: Anything can be identified with the help of probability. Probability determines the chances of occurrence of a particular event in a particular way, out of a number of ways in which the events take place or fail to take place with equal facility.

$$Ps=Ns/Ns+Nf$$

where, Ps represents the probability, Ns represents the no. of ways in which the event can successfully take place, and Nf represents no. of ways in which it fails.

7- Principle of Circumstantial facts: Facts do not lie, Men/Women can and do. It indicates the importance of circumstantial facts than the evidence of eyewitnesses. The testimony of the eyewitness is modified by auto-suggestion, external influence, opinions of others, conscious or unconscious bias, and rationalization.

Forensic science subsists coming together with law and science. Even though forensic science has been identified intimately with the criminal justice system in the past, now the forensic scientist plays a gradually more active role in civil proceedings and in regulatory issues.

Virtually no limitation exists to the scope of physical evidence that is gist for all forensic scientists. Physical evidence may range in size from the microscopic (for example, a pollen grain) to the macroscopic (for example, a diesel truck). This wide meaning covers criminal prosecutions in the widest sense, together with patrons and ecological safeguard and physical condition and protection at work, as well as civil proceeding such as violate of agreement and negligence.

The principles of forensic science guide the disciplines and methodologies of science in analysing the evidence to answer certain questions. These principles of forensic science have an impact upon criminal proceedings which start from the point of investigation upon the occurrence of a crime till the conviction of the accused in the court of law.

1.5 Triangle of Forensic Science

The Triangle of Forensic Science emphasizes the importance of analyzing and interpreting the evidence left behind by the perpetrator, victim, and crime scene to reconstruct the events of the crime. It also underscores the significance of properly collecting, preserving, and analyzing physical evidence to establish connections and draw conclusions in criminal investigations. Forensic Science works to co-relate the evidence with victims and criminals that was recovered after the investigation of the crime scene when the crime is committed. The final report admitted in court is associated with these:

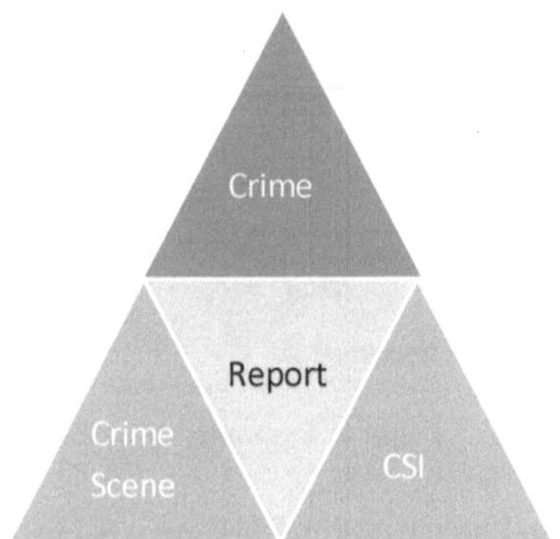

Figure: Triangle of Forensic Science

Crime- Any awful act done by any person, agency, or organization that is harmful to another person, society, or country & that is punishable by law or any other higher authority is a Crime. For example- Robbery, Murder, forgery, etc.

<u>Elements of Crime-</u> The following model describe the crime of conduct and its relationship. The exact definition of crime is a philosophical issue without an agreed-upon answer. Fields such as law, politics, sociology, and psychology define crime in different ways. Crimes may be variously considered as wrongs against individuals, against the community, or against the state. The criminality of an action is dependent on its

context; acts of violence will be seen as crimes in many circumstances but as permissible or desirable in others.

Crime was historically seen as a manifestation of evil, but this has been superseded by modern criminal

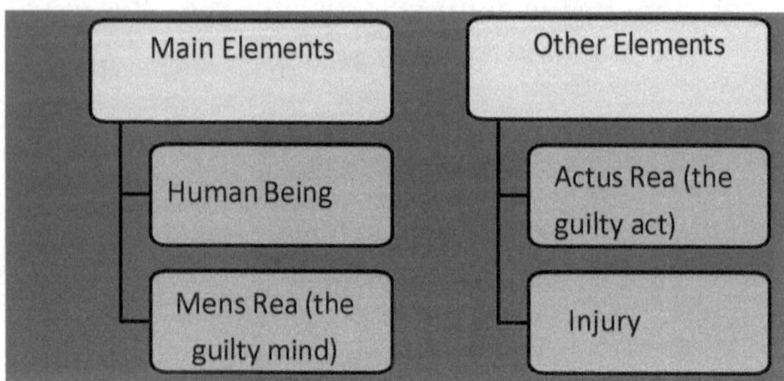

Figure: Elements of Crime

theories. As a sociological concept, crime is associated with actions that cause harm and violate social norms.

Victim- Within the Indian legal framework, the term victim is defined under Section 2(wa) of the CrPC, 1973 as a person who has suffered any loss or injury caused by reason of the act or omission for which the accused person has been charged and the expression victim includes his or her guardian or legal heir.

Culprit- One accused of or charged with a crime. The culprit pleaded "not guilty": one guilty of a crime or a fault.

Eyewitness- A person who has seen something happen and can give a first-hand description of it.

Classification of Crime- Crime has been classified into different catagories according to –

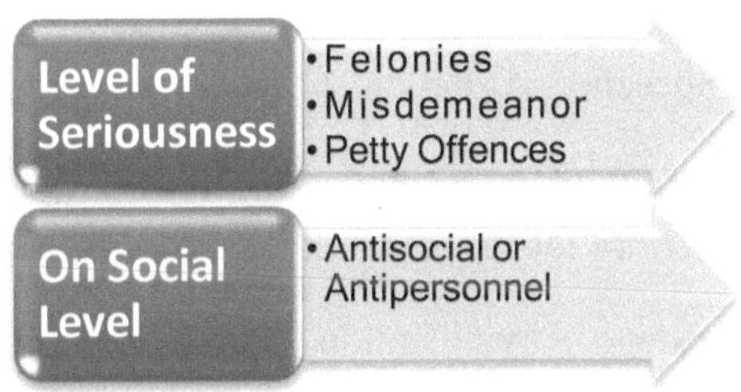

Figure: Classification of Crime

Felonies- Any serious crime that is punishable by more than a year of imprisonment or by death. Eg: Rape, Homicide, etc.

Misdemeanor- Any crime that is less serious and is usually punishable by fines, penalties, or incarceration of less than one year.

Petty Offences- Any insignificant Crime involving very minor misconduct. Eg: Traffic Violation.

Antisocial or Antipersonnel- It is further divided as:

1- Crime against Person. Eg: Sexual offences, Murder, etc.

2- Crime against Moveable or Immoveable possession. Eg: Burgarly, Theft, Robbery, etc.

3- Crime against moral values. Eg: Bribes, Scams, Hacking, Copyrights etc.

4- Crime against Public Peace and Order. Eg: Riots, Hate Speeches, Agitation, etc.

5- Crime against Public Peace and Order. Eg: Riots, Hate Speeches, Agitation, etc.

6- Crime regarding Natural Resources. Eg: Widlife crimes, flora fauna, contaminents, fossils, etc.

Crime Scene- Any location where an offence is committed or suspected to occur is called Crime Scene. The majority of finding physical evidence is more. There are five types of Crime Scenes:

1- Primary Crime Scene- Locale where crime is actually committed.

2- Secondary Crime Scene- Locale where related evidences are found.

3- Indoor Crime Scene- Crime occur within a roof.

4- Outdoor Crime Scene- Crime occur in open area.

5- Mobile Crime Scene- Crime committed in a moving phase.

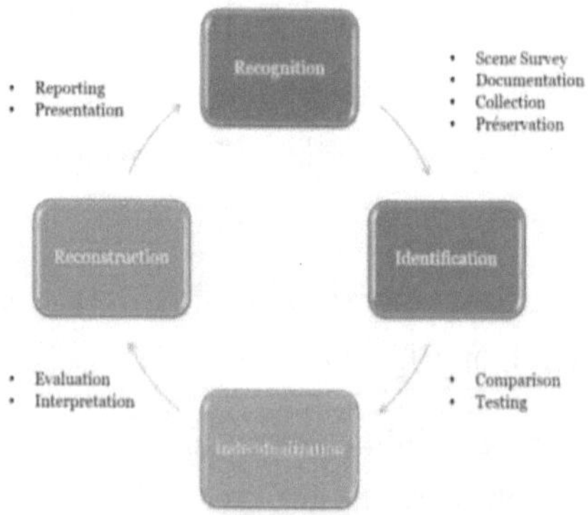

Figure: Scientific Examination of Crime Scene

Crime Scene Investigation- CSI is a multidisciplinary process that involves systematic search & meticulous observation of the crime scene by a dedicated group of forensic investigators. The importance of CSI is to establish whether a crime is committed or not & to identify the sequence of events that happened during the crime. This technical process also helps to recover physical evidence that is sent to Forensic Laboratories For further examination to solve the mystery. The procedure acquired to investigate the crime:

CHAIN OF CUSTODY (COC)

It is the chronological documentation or paper trial that records the sequence of custody, control, transfer, analysis, and disposition of materials,

Crime reconstruction or crime scene reconstruction is the forensic science discipline in which one gains "explicit knowledge of the series of events that surround the commission of a crime using deductive and inductive reasoning, physical evidence, scientific methods, and their interrelationships". It is important to note that crime scene reconstruction is a complex and multidisciplinary process that requires expertise in various forensic disciplines. It relies on the integration of scientific analysis, logical reasoning, and investigative techniques to provide a comprehensive understanding of the crime and assist in the pursuit of justice.

The processing of Crime Scene consists of several steps including: securing the scene, documenting the scene, collecting and transportation of evidences, examining the evidences for making final report.

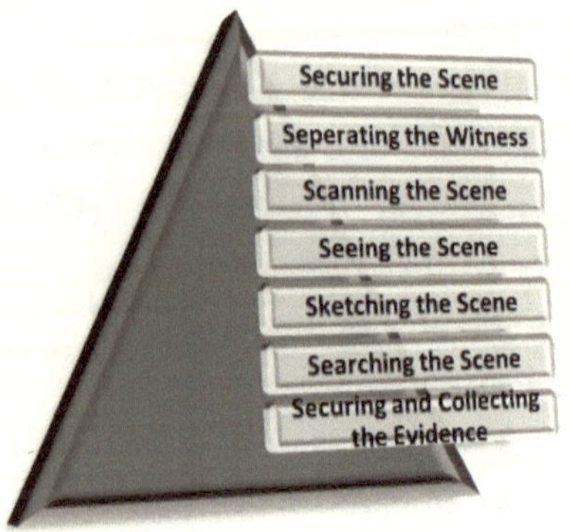

Figure: Seven S' (7 S') of Crime Scene Investigation

Crime Scene Documentation- The purpose of crime scene documentation is to permanently record the condition of the crime scene and its physical evidence. It is the most time-consuming activity at the scene and requires the investigator to stay organized and systematic. Problem-solving skills, innovation, and originality will also be needed. The four major tasks of documentation are:

1- Notetaking: This includes information of arrival date and time, scene description along with weather, location type and condition, identification of transient & conditional evidence, clothing, and any weapons present. Victim description also be noted with position of victim, wounds, clothing, jewellery, or identification. Crime scene team noted walk-through information, beginning and ending times, and evidence.

2- Videography- Video recording of crime scenes is a valuable tool for providing an overall, accurate impression of the crime scene that often cannot be accomplished by the other documentation tasks; however, it is never an adequate substitute for any of the other tasks. Also record the victim's viewpoint.

3- Photography- The following is the basic equipment needed for photographic documentation of crime scene that includes Camera (35 mm is the most common type), Normal lens (50 to 60 mm), Wide angle lens (28 to 35 mm), Electronic flash with cord Tripod. There are three 3 general categories of photographs: **Overview** - gives general locale and approach route. **Mid-range** - mid-range (10-20 feet) tell a story that helps establish the modus operandi (MO)of the offender. **Close-up** - essential for establishing the corpus delicti of a criminal act. There are two 2 general methods of photography: **Overlapping**: which is a series of photos taken in a circular or clockwise direction, overlapping each slightly to show the overall scene. **Progressive**: which starts from a fixed point, photographs each piece of evidence as the photographer moves toward it, and progressively gets closer in the pictures.

4- Sketching- Sketching a crime scene is the assignment of units of measurement or correct perspective to the overall screen and the relevant physical evidence identified within the scene. There are two types of Sketches of the crime scenes: Rough sketches and finished or final sketches. **Objectives of sketches:** Present a clear "mind's eye" picture of the crime scene. Complement investigator's notes and photos. Show accurate location and relationships of the evidence items. Refresh the memory of investigators. Illustrate the testimony of witnesses. Provide factual data for crime scene reconstructions.

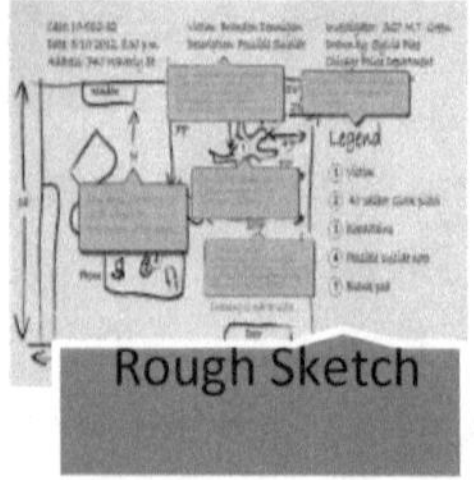

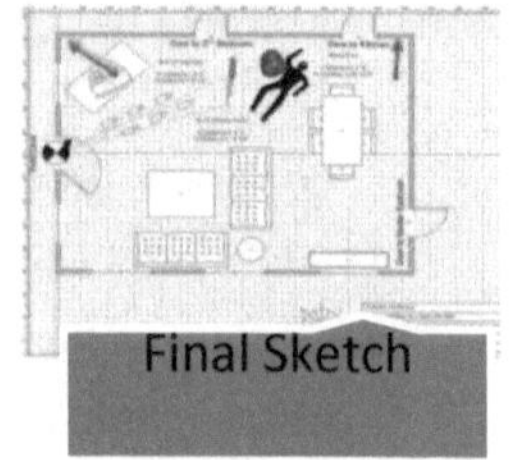

Figure: Types of Sketches

<u>Searching the Crime Scene</u>- After completion of the crime scene documentation and intensive search of the scene for physical evidence, the collection and preservation of the evidence can begin.

Three Golden Rules to maximize the recovery of evidence: Search area should be determined to maximize concentration. Each area should no more than 20-40 minutes to search. Breaks should be taken after each search. (at least 10 mins). Search the same area twice so that nothing is overlooked.

There are various types of Searching methods but mostly used are –

Zone Method: The Zone search method divide the area to be searched in half or in quarters. These areas can be subdivided into quadrants if needed. This pattern can be used in small outdoor scenes but work best on interior room searches and when searching vehicles.

Figure: Zone Search Method

Line Method: The Lane or Line search method is a good search pattern for outdoor scenes. At large scenes begin with six or seven lanes. This method is suited for the crime scene like class rooms, where rows are present already, each row is considered as a strip.

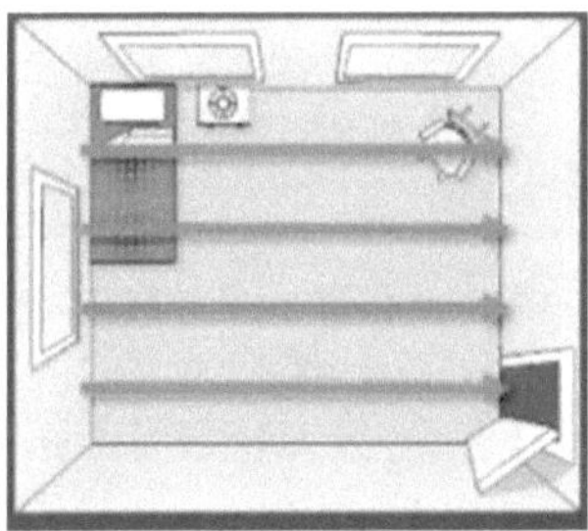

Figure: Line Search Method

Spiral Method: This method is typically used for outdoor scenes. This search pattern is usually conducted by a single searcher who walks in a slightly decreasing, less-than-concentric circle from the outermost boundary towards the centre for certain crimes.

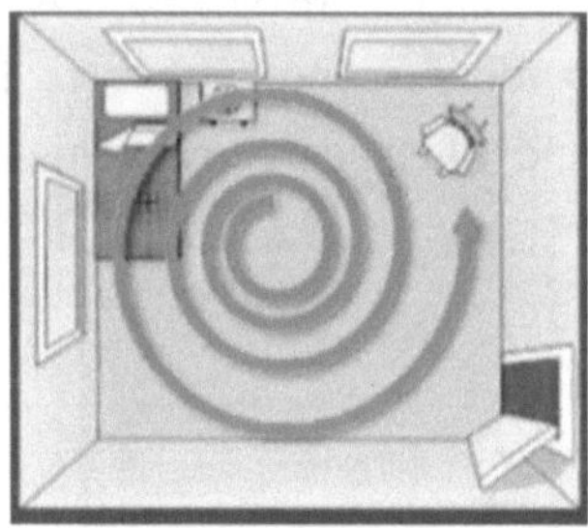

Figure: Spiral Search Method

Grid Method: The grid search is a useful search pattern at outdoor scenes. The grids should be kept to a size 10'x10' or 12'x12' so that a complete and thorough search is performed.

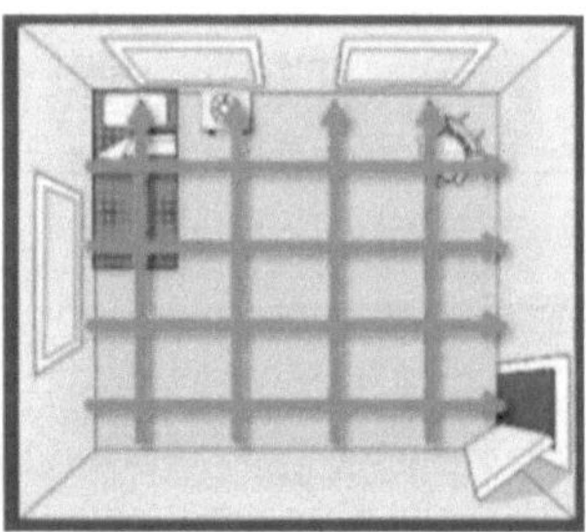

Figure: Grid Search Method

Wheel Method: The pie or wheel search is a pattern that is especially useful at bombing scenes. The centre of the pie or wheel can be anything and the outer perimeter will be the distance from the centre to the outer most piece of evidence plus one-half the total distance.

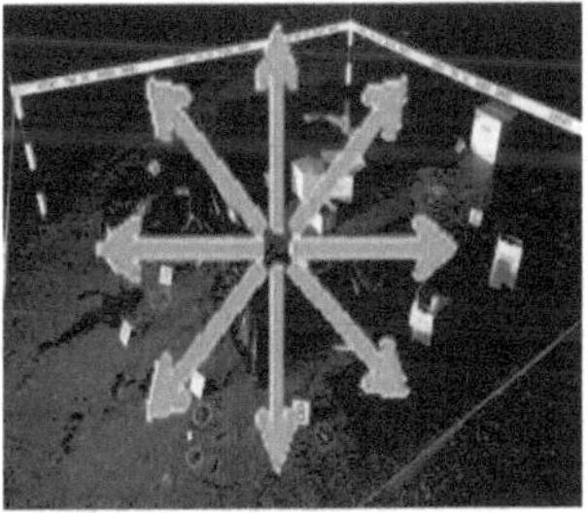

Figure: Wheel Search Method

<u>Collection and Preservation</u>- Evidence collection procedure should be performed in a systematic and careful manner. The process begins with the preliminary crime scene survey, followed by a searching of the evidences and its collection. The sequence of evidence collection involves following basis:

▫The crime scene location: interior, exterior, within a vehicle.

▫The evidence condition: either fragile or stable.

▫Scene management considerations which may alter or contaminate the evidence.

All the evidences packaged are marked following information:

- ▫ Case number.
- ▫ Evidence number.
- ▫ Description of the Evidence (s).

- Investigator's name or initials.
- Signature of the Investigator
- Date of the collection

Transportation- This last phase of the crime scene investigation process aims at selecting the means of transportation which is appropriate for the type of physical evidence to ensure the integrity of evidence submitted to the laboratory. The transportation to the laboratory location prior to examination of the evidence is a crucial step. Adequate conditions, e.g. a cool and dry place, and secured and controlled access are essential characteristics of transport and storage conditions. Documentation of transportation, storage and hand-over to the laboratory is important. A written receipt is usually issued for all evidence submitted to the laboratory.

Report- A forensic report simply and succinctly summarizes the substantive evidence in a criminal case. Forensic report writing may prove difficult and daunting because it usually demands analyses of technical data, presented in a readable, easy-to-follow format. Nevertheless, a forensic report essentially follows the same basic standards and protocols required of any report.

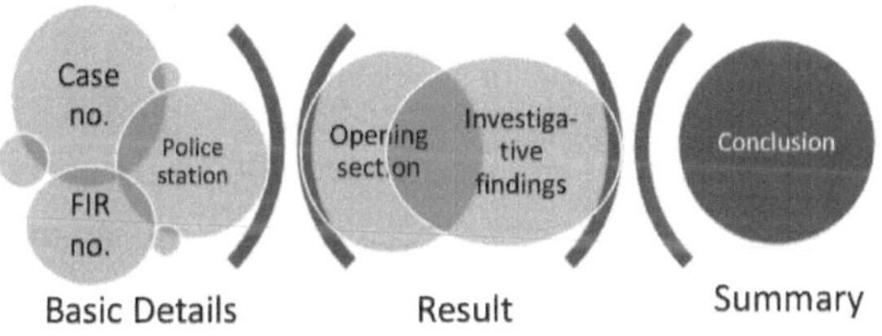

Figure: Format of Report

1.6 Forensic Science Laboratories

A crime laboratory, also called forensic laboratory (FSL), facility where analyses are performed on evidence generated by crime or, sometimes, civil infractions. Crime laboratories can investigate physical, chemical, biological, or digital evidence and often employ specialists in a variety of disciplines, including behavioural forensic science, forensic pathology, forensic anthropology, crime-scene investigation, and ballistics Many crime labs are publicly funded and administered by federal, state or provincial, or local government. Forensic scientists- also play an important part. They will take samples collected at the scene and analyze them in a forensics laboratory. With a little ingenuity and some very high-tech equipment, forensic scientists can help law enforcement catch even the wiliest perpetrator. They analyze and interpret evidence found at the crime scene. That evidence can include blood, saliva, fibers, tire tracks, drugs, alcohol, paint chips and firearm residue. Using scientific equipment, forensic scientists identify the components of the samples and match them up. While some forensic scientists travel to the scene of the crime to collect the evidence themselves, others occupy a laboratory role, performing analysis on objects brought to them by other individuals. Still others are involved in analysis of financial, banking, or other numerical data for use in financial crime investigation, and can be employed as consultants from private firms, academia, or as government employees.

1.6.1 Forensic Laboratories in India-

The Central Forensic Science Laboratory (CFSL) is a wing of the Indian Ministry of Home Affairs, which fulfills the forensic requirements in the country. There are six CFSLs of the Directorate of Forensic Science Services (DFSS) in the country located at Bhopal, Chandigarh, Guwahati, Hyderabad, Kolkata & Pune. One more Central Forensic Science Laboratory (7th) is under the control of the Central Bureau of Investigation (CBI) located in New Delhi.

Figure: CFSLs of India under DFSS

In India, there are 31 State Forensic Science Laboratories devoted to serving different Indian States.

1. Kerala Forensic Science Laboratory
2. Jharkhand State Forensic Science Laboratory
3. Chhattisgarh State Forensic Science Laboratory
4. Goa State Forensic Science Laboratory
5. Tamil Nadu Forensic Science Laboratory
6. Madhya Pradesh State Forensic Science Laboratory
7. Rajasthan State Forensic Science Laboratory
8. Tripura State Forensic Science Laboratory
9. Karnataka State Forensic Science Laboratory
10. Maharashtra State Forensic Science Laboratory
11. Himachal Pradesh State Forensic Science Laboratory
12. Meghalaya State Forensic Science Laboratory
13. Telangana State Forensic Science Laboratory
14. Gujarat State Forensic Science Laboratory
15. Punjab State Forensic Science Laboratory
16. Arunachal Pradesh State Forensic Science Laboratory
17. Jammu & Kashmir State

The OCME Department of Forensic Biology operates the largest public DNA crime laboratory in the world.

Forensic Science Laboratory

18. Andaman & Nicobar Forensic Science Laboratory
19. Haryana State Forensic Science Laboratory
20. Andhra Pradesh State Forensic Science Laboratory
21. Uttar Pradesh State Forensic Science Laboratory
22. Delhi State Forensic Science Laboratory
23. Assam State Forensic Science Laboratory
24. Manipur State Forensic Science Laboratory
25. Puducherry Forensic Science Laboratory
26. Odisha State Forensic Science Laboratory
27. Bihar State Forensic Science Laboratory
28. West Bengal State Forensic Science Laboratory
29. Mizoram State Forensic Science Laboratory
30. Nagaland State Forensic Science Laboratory
31. Uttarakhand State Forensic Science Laboratory

1.6.2 History of Forensic Laboratory –

The history of Forensic Science is thousands of years old in India. Kautilya mentioned about study of pupillary line pattern in his "Artha shastra".

Year of Establishment	FSL
1849	1st Chemical Examination Lab,

	Chennai
1853	2nd Chemical Examination Lab, Kolkata
1864	3rd Chemical Examination Lab, Agra
1870	4th Chemical Examination, Mumbai
1892	1st Anthropometry Bureau, Kolkata
1898	1st Explosive Lab, Nagpur
1904	1st Government Examiner QuestionDocument (GEQD), Bengal
1906	GEQD shifted to Shimla
1910	Serology Lab, Kolkata by Dr. Hankin
1952	1st SFSL, Calcutta
1957	1st CFSL, Calcutta and Fingerprint Bureau by Khan Bahadur Aziz ulla & Ray BahadurKhem Chandra Bose
1960	Indian Academy of Forensic Science(IAFS)

Table: History of FSL's in India

1.7 Branches of Forensic Science

Ful service crime labs offer a variety of basic services and many also provide optional services as well. The physical science unit applies the principles and techniques of chemistry, physics, and geology to the identification and comparison of crime-scene evidence. Expert criminalists staff this unit and use modern analytical instrumentation for a diverse examination of evidence. Following are the branches of Forensic Science:

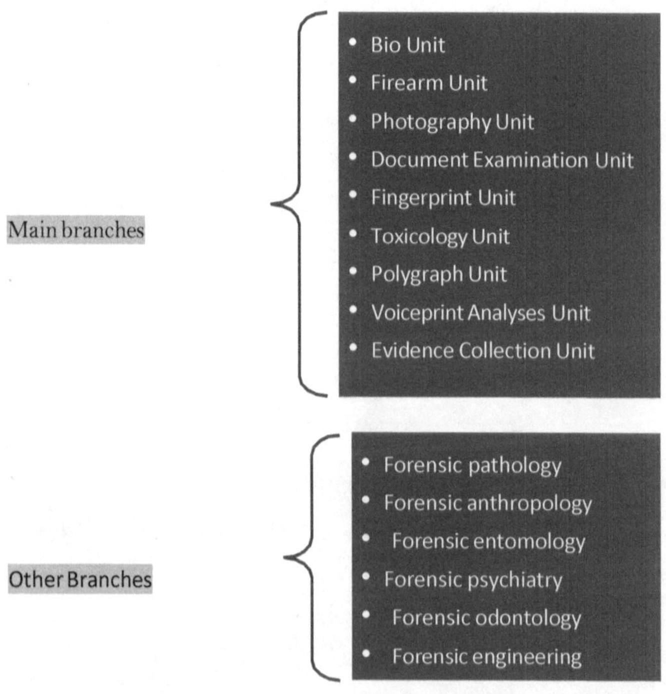

Figure: Division in FSL

A **biology unit** is staffed with biochemists and biologists that apply techniques to identify DNA profiling, blood, and other body fluids. They also examine hairs, fibers, wood, and plants.

The **firearms unit** is a busy place due to the number of firearms used in crimes. They also study discharged bullets, cartridges cases, shotgun shells, and ammunition of all types. The comparison of tool marks is also examined at this unit.

The **photography unit** examines and records physical evidence. Highly specialized technology aids in the preparation of photographic exhibits for courtroom presentation.

At the **document examination** unit handwriting and typewriting on questioned documents are studied to ascertain authenticity and/or the source.

The **latent fingerprinting** unit processes and examines evidence for latent fingerprints.

The **toxicology unit** examines body fluids and organs to determine the presence or absence of drugs and poisons.

In the **polygraph unit**, or lie detector, the staff is trained in the techniques of criminal investigation and interrogation. The lie detector has become to be recognized as an essential tool of the criminal investigator rather than the forensic scientist.

In the **voiceprint analysis unit** investigators tie the voice to a particular suspect. A sound spectrograph is used that transform speech into a visual graphic display called a voiceprint. Sound patterns produced in speech are unique to the individual and this validity provides the uniqueness of the speech patterns.

The **evidence collection unit** incorporates crime-scene evidence collection into the total forensic science is slowly gaining recognition in the U.S. The unit dispatches specially trained personnel to the crime scene to collect and preserve physical evidence that will later be processed at the crime lab.

Other forensic services offered at a full-service crime lab might include: forensic pathology, anthropology, entomology, psychiatry, odontology, and engineering. This is by no means a complete list of services provided by a crime laboratory. The various units and their services will be discussed in detail in future content of this course.

Forensic pathology is a subspecialty of pathology that investigates non-natural or suspicious deaths, often referred to as reportable deaths. Forensic pathology focuses on determining the cause of death via postmortem examinations or autopsies.

Forensic anthropology is the examination of human skeletal remains for law enforcement agencies to help with the recovery of human remains, determine the identity of unidentified human remains, interpret trauma, and estimate time since death.

Forensic entomology is the scientific study of the colonization of a dead body by arthropods. This includes the study of insect types commonly associated with cadavers, their respective life cycles, their ecological presences in a given environment, as well as the changes in insect assemblage with the progression of decomposition.

Forensic psychiatry is defined as a sub-branch of psychiatry. It deals with patients and issues at the interface of the legal and psychiatric systems applied to legal issues in context to legislative matters.

Forensic Odontology is the field of dentistry in which dental knowledge is applied to questions of law. It is a subspecialty of dentistry that has as its main focus on the identification of deceased persons.

Forensic engineering is the process of investigating and collecting data related to the: materials, products, structures or components that failed. It includes the investigation of materials and products.

Some other important branches:

- Forensic intelligence process starts with the collection of data and ends with the integration of results within into the analysis of crimes under investigation.

- Forensic histopathology is the application of histological techniques and examination to forensic pathology practice. Wildlife forensic science applies a range of scientific disciplines to legal cases involving non-human biological evidence, to solve crimes such as poaching, animal abuse, and trade in endangered species.

- Forensic seismology is the study of techniques to distinguish the seismic signals generated by underground nuclear explosions from those generated by earthquakes.

1.8 Organization Structure of Forensic Science Laboratory

The organizational structure of forensic laboratories can vary depending on the specific jurisdiction, size of the lab, and the types of services it provides. However, there are some common elements and positions found in many forensic laboratories. Here is a general overview of the typical organizational structure:

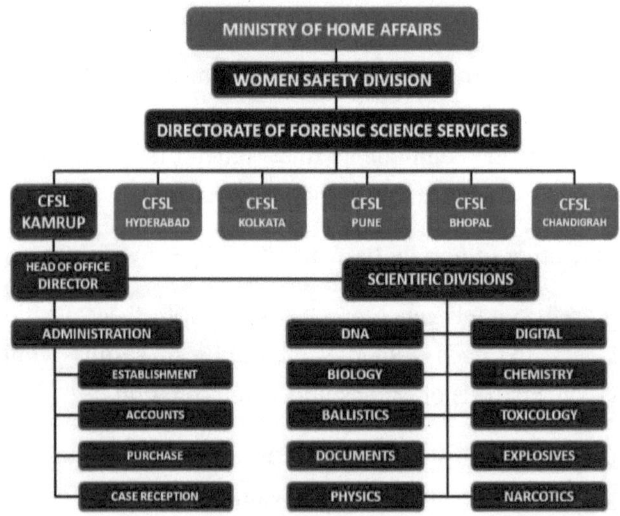

Figure: Hierarchy with divisions in CFSL

Director
Additional Director
Deputy Director
Assistant Director
Senior Scientific Officer (SSO)
Scientific Officer (SO)
Senior Scientific Assistant (SSA)
Scientific Assistant (SA)
Lab Assistant (LA)
Lab Attendant
Receptionist/Sweeper/Peon/Helper

Figure: Lab Administration Hierarchy

The organizational structure may differ between public and private forensic laboratories, and some positions may have different titles or additional roles depending on the specific lab's needs and resources. The structure may also include specialized units or divisions based on the specific forensic disciplines or services offered by the laboratory. Training and Development: This unit is responsible for the training and professional development of laboratory personnel. They develop and deliver training programs, organize workshops and seminars, and ensure staff members stay updated on the latest advancements in their respective fields.

BIOLOGICAL EVIDENCES

Epilogue

Forensic biology division deals with the examination of biological fluids, skeletal remnants, diatoms, hair, seeds, maggots, etc. present in various items of evidentiary value in crime cases such as murder, attempt to murder, sexual assault and child abuse.

The division is equipped with the state-of-art technologies and expertise to carry out all types of analytical works related to forensic biology. The biological analysis includes detection and establishment of any biological fluids like blood, semen, saliva, urine, sweat, milk, fibre, tissue and botanical exhibits. Further, the laboratory has been upgrading to carryout accurate microscopic examinations.

Most often, these fluids are analyzed for their presence so that DNA can be extracted from it (in DNA division), and thus may link a suspect to a crime scene.

Predominantly, it includes the examination of:

1- Semen

2- Saliva

3- Sweat

2.1 Semen

Semen is a combination of seminal fluids from the prostate gland, seminal vesicle, epididymis, and bulbourethral glands along with sperm (spermatozoa). They are capable of fertilizing the female's eggs.

Ph of Semen: 7.2-7.

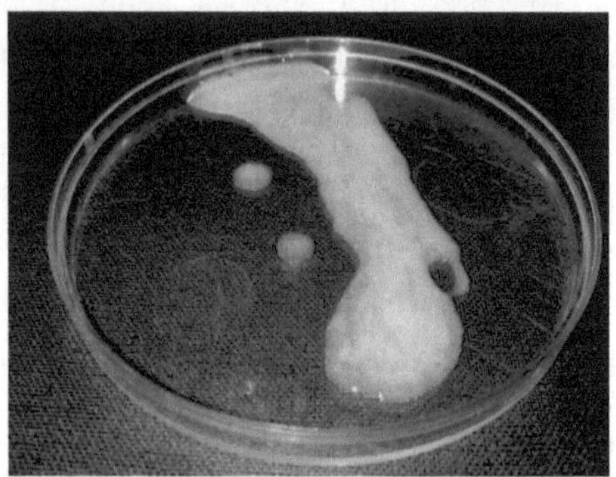

Figure: Human Semen

Semen can be stored in diluents such as the Illini Variable Temperature (IVT) diluent, which have been reported to be able to preserve high fertility of semen for over seven days. The IVT diluent is composed of several salts, sugars and antibacterial agents and gassed with CO2.

Composition of Semen- Seminal Vesical: Secrets Choline & Fructose. Prostate Gland: Secrets P30 enzyme, Spermine & Acid Phosphate Enzyme. Cowper's Gland: Secrets Yellowish pigmentation, Lubrication. Testes: Secrets Sperms.

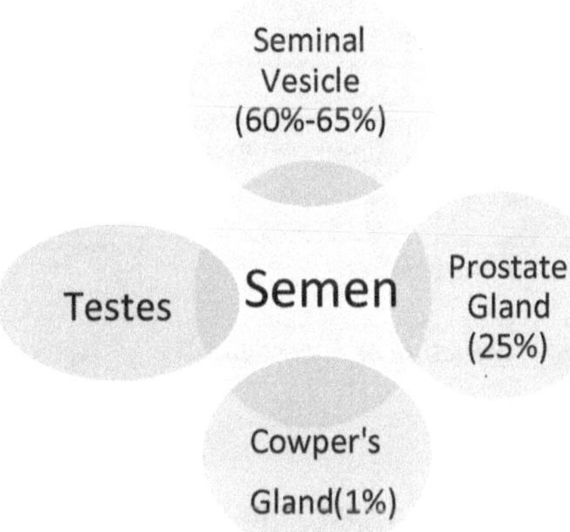

Figure: Composition of Semen with acquired percentage

Sperm- Also called Spermatozoa & around 200-300 million sperms are ejaculated at once.

STRUCTURE: Consist of three parts Head, Middle Piece, Tail.

1. Head- Contains acrosome apically, which, contains, enzymes, that, facilitate, entry of sperm, into the ovum. It has genetical material.

2. Middle piece- Contains mitochondria, which known as power house of the cell.

3. Tail- It is a flagellum that produce out of the cell body and is responsible for the vigorous motality of sperms. It helps the sperm to swim so that they can reach towards the ovum.

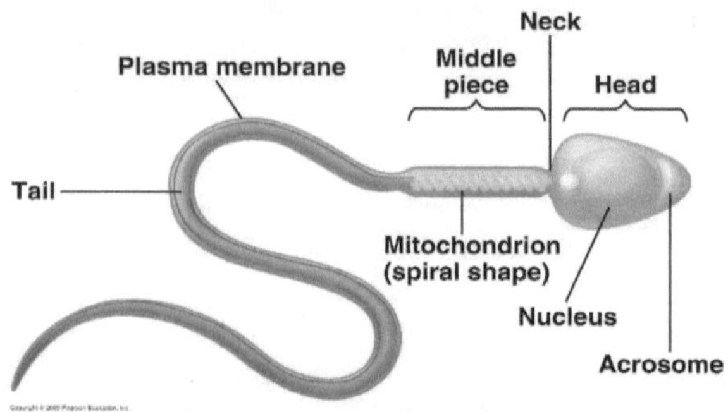

Figure: Structure of Spermatozoa

Spermatogenesis

Spermatogenesis is the process by which haploid spermatozoa develop from germ cells in the seminiferous tubules of the testis. This process starts with the mitotic division of the stem cells located close to the basement membrane of the tubules.

These cells are called spermatogonial stem cells. The mitotic division of these produces two types of cells. Type A cells replenish the stem cells, and type B cells differentiate into primary spermatocytes. The primary spermatocyte divides meiotically (Meiosis I) into two secondary spermatocytes; each secondary spermatocyte divides into two equal haploid spermatids by Meiosis II.

The spermatids are transformed into spermatozoa (sperm) by the process of spermiogenesis. These develop into mature spermatozoa, also known as sperm cells. Thus, the primary spermatocyte gives rise to two cells, the secondary spermatocytes, and the two secondary spermatocytes by their subdivision produce four spermatozoa and four haploid cells.

Spermatozoa are the mature male gametes in many sexually reproducing organisms. Thus, spermatogenesis is the male version of gametogenesis, of which the female equivalent is oogenesis. In mammals it occurs in the seminiferous tubules of the male testes in a stepwise fashion. Spermatogenesis is highly dependent upon optimal conditions for the process to occur correctly, and is essential for sexual reproduction.

DNA methylation and histone modification have been implicated in the regulation of this process. It starts during puberty and usually continues uninterrupted until death, although a slight decrease can be discerned in the quantity of produced sperm with increase in age.

Spermatogenesis starts in the bottom part of seminiferous tubes and, progressively, cells go deeper into tubes and moving along it until mature spermatozoa reaches the lumen, where mature spermatozoa are deposited.

The division happens asynchronically; if the tube is cut transversally, one could observe different maturation states. A group of cells with different maturation states that are being generated at the same time is called a spermatogenic wave.

- Duration- For humans, the entire process of spermatogenesis is variously estimated as taking 74 days (according to tritium-labelled biopsies) and approximately 120 days (according to DNA clock measurements). Including the transport on ductal system, it takes 3 months. Testes produce 200 to 300 million spermatozoa daily. However, only about half or 100 million of these become viable sperm.

• Location in Humans- Spermatogenesis takes place within several structures of the male reproductive system. The initial stages occur within the testes and progress to the epididymis where the developing gametes mature and are stored until ejaculation. The seminiferous tubules of the testes are the starting point for the process, where spermatogonial stem cells adjacent to the inner tubule wall divide in a centripetal direction—beginning at the walls and proceeding into the innermost part, or lumen—to produce immature sperm. Maturation occurs in the epididymis. The location [Testes/Scrotum] is specifically important as the process of spermatogenesis requires a lower temperature to produce viable sperm, specifically 1°-8 °C lower than normal body temperature of 37 °C (98.6 °F). Clinically, small fluctuations in temperature such as from an athletic support strap, causes no impairment in sperm viability or count.

• Disorders- Spermatogenesis may cause oligospermia, which is semen with a low concentration of sperm and is a common finding in male infertility.

Here is a general overview of the stages involved in spermatogenesis: Germ Cell Division (Mitosis): The process begins with the division of germ cells called spermatogonia. These cells are located in the seminiferous tubules of the testes. Some spermatogonia remain as stem cells for self-renewal, while others differentiate into primary spermatocytes.

Meiosis I: Primary spermatocytes undergo the first meiotic division, resulting in the formation of two secondary spermatocytes. This division reduces the chromosome number from diploid (46 chromosomes) to haploid (23 chromosomes) in each cell.

Meiosis II: Each secondary spermatocyte further undergoes the second meiotic division, resulting in the formation of four haploid spermatids.

Spermiogenesis: Spermatids undergo a series of morphological changes during spermiogenesis to develop into mature sperm cells (spermatozoa). These changes involve the formation of a head, midpiece, and tail.

Sperm Maturation: The immature sperm cells (spermatids) are released from the seminiferous tubules into the epididymis, where they undergo maturation. This maturation process involves acquiring motility and the ability to fertilize an egg.

Semen as Evidence- Semen is an invaluable sample that can provide information on who may have executed an unwarranted sex act. It is mostly found in the cases like Sodomy, rape, bestiality, lust murders. Semen can indeed be a valuable forensic tool in solving certain types of crimes, particularly those involving sexual assault. Semen contains DNA, which can be used to identify and link individuals to a crime scene. DNA profiling techniques can compare the DNA found in semen samples with the DNA profiles of potential suspects, victims, or other samples in a DNA database, helping to establish connections or exclusions.

It is important to note that while semen analysis can provide valuable evidence in certain cases, it is just one piece of the puzzle in a criminal investigation. Other types of evidence, such as fingerprints, witness testimonies, or surveillance footage, are often needed to build a complete picture and reach a conclusion in a criminal case.

Forensic scientists can extract semen from various surfaces, such as clothing, bedding, or the victim's body, and perform DNA analysis on the sample. If a suspect is identified, their DNA can be compared to the DNA from the semen sample to determine if there is a match.

The key lies in identifying a sample. The procedure includes proper **Collection, Preservation, Packaging** discussed below:

Collection: Collection of semen stain has much precaution. Semen converts in to brittle after drying. So, if cloths or other articles are not handled properly or folded it then spermatozoa are breakdown in to pieces.

- Commonly, semen is found on bedsheets, cloths, undergarments, condoms (if used) carpets, or the floor where crime is occurred.

• Most stains are visible due to the characteristic off-white to yellow, crusty appearance against a dark background. Stains on light surfaces may need to be revealed using light sources such as blue lights or ultraviolet lights. When samples are exposed to these lights, a seminal stain will fluoresce.

• Finding sperm cells in body cavities of a victim of sexual crime is the utmost priority for obvious reasons. Several research findings indicate that motile and non motile sperms can be obtained at different duration in different body cavities.

• A dry sample on clothing or bedding needs to be rubbed gently to release any intact sperm or may be immersed and agitated in water. If rubbed too hard, the chances of the cells breaking apart will be great. Sometimes, a sperm sample may be bound so tight to clothing that immersing it in water will not release the individual cells.

Preservation & Packaging: Preservation of semen stain always performed after complete dryness of stain. If stain is wet then bacterial growth is started and putrefaction may occur due to presence of protein in semen.

• Any infection in testis due to presence of some bacteria also secretes liquid like seminal stain from testis which creates doubt about semen. It is always preserved in air bag not in airtight bag or plastic bag.

• If stain found on immovable or small article, then preserved whole article or cloth and sent sample to FSL.

• If stain present on immovable article then sharp knife or scalpel is used to scratch the stain and packed in clean glass bottle.

• Seminal stain may be present on pubic hair so it is also preserved in bag or clean plastic tube.

• If seminal stain present on any body part then take cotton swab is taken, dipped in saline water. Then cotton applies on body and prepare cotton swab. After that drying the cotton swab and preserved in bag.

• In fresh seminal stain, live spermatozoa are present so keep safe the cloth and send properly to FSL.

• Semen cryopreservation can be used for far longer storage durations. For human sperm, the longest reported successful storage with this method is 21 years.

• There are instances that will reduce counts of semen such as medical issues, diet, age, and illegal and legal drug use. Males may produce lower than normal counts of sperm, which is known as oligospermia. A male may also be infertile, producing no sperm, a situation known as aspermia. Males that have had a vasectomy, which is a procedure to sever the vas deferens to prevent the transfer of sperm, will also produce ejaculations that are absent of semen.

First, the screening tests are performed in order to identify whether the questioned stain is semen or not.

Once the preliminary screening tests are positive, a more detailed confirmatory analysis is carried out to establish that the stain is indeed semen. Further exhaustive analysis of seminal stains is performed in order to individualize the stain to a particular individual in DNA division.

	Vagina	Cervix	Mouth	Rectum	Anus
Motile Sperms	6-28 h	3-7.5 days	--	--	--
Non-Motile Sperms	14 h – 10 days	7.5-19 days	2-31 h	4-113 h	2-44 h

Table: Approximate duration of motile and non-motile sperms found in the body cavities

The identification of one or more sperms is a conclusive proof of the presence of semen can be determined by following examinations:

• Physical Examination- In this we examine colour, texture, and odour.

Colour- Grey, Whitish

Texture- Starch like solution

Odour- Pungent smell

• Other examination- Chemicals and microscopes are used to examine that includes:

Presumptive Test- Acid Phosphate Test, Barberio's Test Florence Test, P30 Test.

Confirmatory Test- Microscopic Examination, Christmas Tree Test, Methylene Blue Test, Hemalum Test.

Presumptive Test for Semen

Acid Phosphate Test: Acid phosphatase is an enzyme present in seminal fluid in concentration far more than that found in any other body fluid. In this catalysis of hydrolysis of phosphate happen.

An extract of the suspected stain is treated with an acidic solution of alpha naphthyl phosphate followed by bentamine Fast Blue B dye. The appearance of intense purple color will determine the presence of acid phosphatase enzyme in the semen stain.

• Reagent Preparations

Step 1. Reagent -Buffer – 50ml Sodium alpha-naphthyl Phosphate, 0.25% (w/v) – 126gm

Step 2. Reagent Buffer- 50ml Naphthanil diazo blue B, 0.5% (w/v) – 250gm

• Procedure: Reaction time is less than 30 sec is a strong indication of semen.

1- Place a small piece (2 x 2 mm) of suspected seminal stain

2- Stain material on Whattman filter paper or other suitable test paper. Use proper standards and controls including positive, negative and unstained controls.

3- Add 1-2 drops of Step 1 Reagent and allow to react for 30 seconds. (No colour should develop at this stage)

4- Add 1drop of Step 2 Reagent. Record the result after 10 seconds. A positive reaction is recorded upon rapid development of a purple colour, which is indicative of semen.

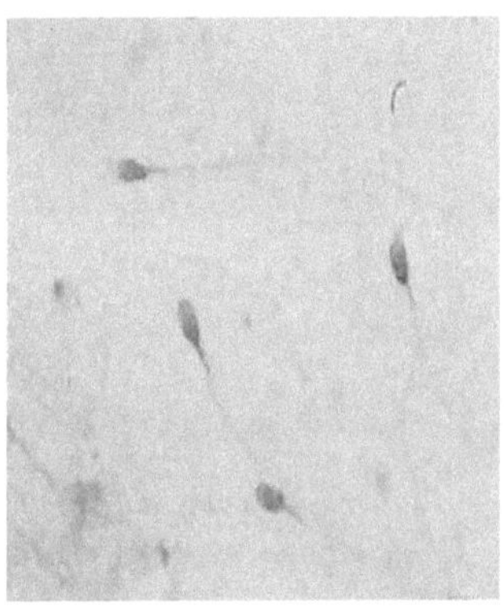

Figure: Purple colour indicating the presence of semen

Time	Semen
24hrs	138 (sigma/ml)
48hrs	50(sigma/ml)
not semen	20(sigma/ml)

Table: Quantity of semen detect time since intercourse

Barberio's Test: Barberio's test was invented by Barberio in the year 1905. When the questioned stain is allowed to react with picric acid it leads to the formation of yellow needle-shaped of spermine picrate crystals, including the presence of seminal stain. It basically detects spermine in the questioned stain.

Figure: Yellow needle crystals indicating presence of spermine

Florence Test: This test was discovered by Dr. Florence in the year 1886. When Florence reagent (Potassium+ Iodide+ Water) is applied to the slide it produces rhomboidal shape dark brown crystals of choline periodide.

Similarly, any tissue or biological material containing sufficient high choline concentration would give positive Florence Test. Sometimes this test gives false positive test in postmortem vaginal swab.

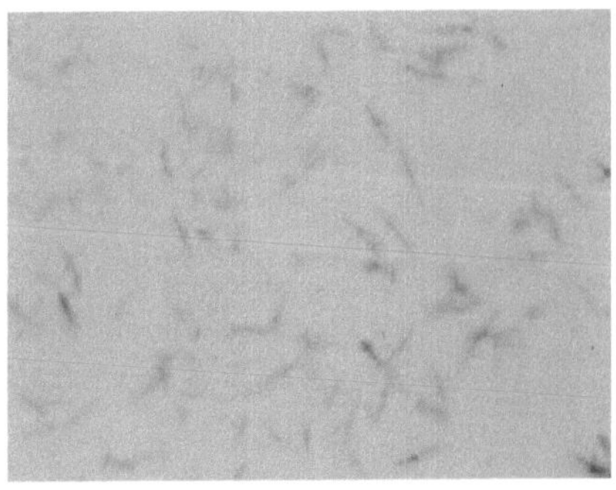

Figure: Dark brown crystals indicating choline in semen

P30: Also known as ABA card test. P30 detects. The test contains an antibody that reacts with p30 in seminal fluid. If the antibody and antigen come together, they will produce pink bands in the testing area. Two bands (one for the control and one for the actual test) show a positive result, whereas one band (the control should always have a band present to indicate that the test strip is actually working) will show a negative result. The ABA card is sensitive to dilutions of 1:2048-8192 and the cost for each test is very favorable. Sometimes there may be other substances that contain PSA, such as breast milk, but in much smaller amounts. Although this test is sensitive to great dilutions of PSA found in semen, its specificity may be a drawback. PSA can persist in the vaginal cavity for only up to twenty-four hours. The earlier the sample is taken, the better the result.

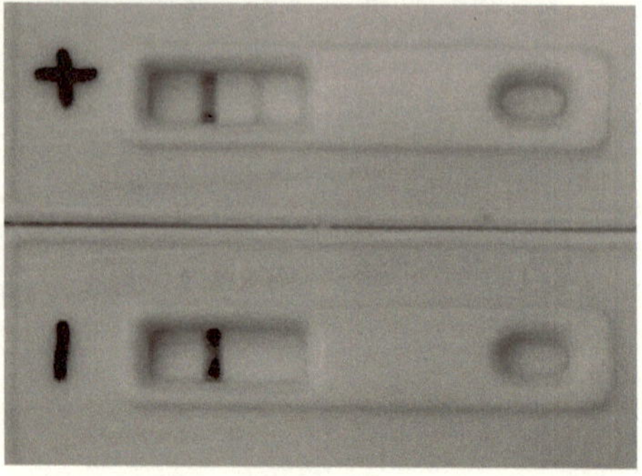

Figure: Two pink line indicates the presence of semen

Confirmatory Test for Semen

Microscopic Examination: Semen can be conclusively identified by the presence of spermatozoa in the stain. When the stain is subjected to a microscopic examination, spermatozoa can be identified as having been derived from semen. Spermatozoa contain gram-positive protein, the presence of spermatozoa will be confirmed by the microscopic appearance of purple bodies.

Christmas Tree Test: The sample is extracted with sterile water in order to make a wet mount on a microscope slide. The sample is then heat-fixed to the slide and stained with Nuclear Fast Red for 15 minutes, then rinsed with deionized water. Next, Picro Indigo Carmine (a green stain) is applied for 10 seconds, then rinsed with ethanol. The slide is placed under a compound light microscope for sperm observation.

If sperm are present, the following observations will appear:

- tip of the head – pink due to fast red dye
- bottom of the head – dark red due to fast red dye
- middle piece – blue due to picro indigo carmine
- tail – yellowish green due to picro indigo carmine
- stem cells – bluish green

Figure: Christmas Tree Stain

Methylene Blue Test: The questioned stain is put on a glass slide and then of methylene blue added to stain. After 30 min, on adding eosin to the slide, Body portion stained with black and head portion remains unstained.

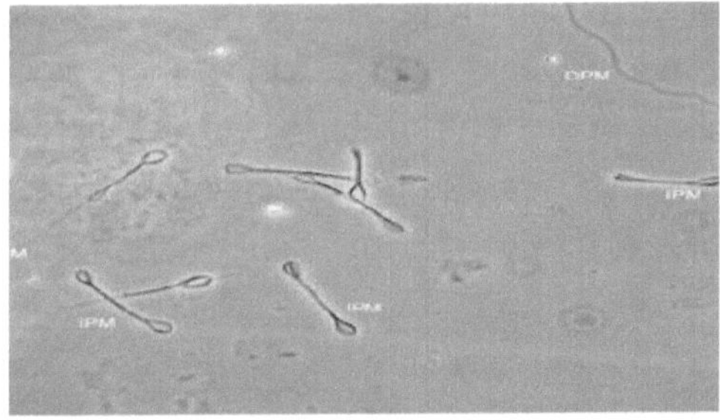

Figure: Methylene Blue Staining

Hemalum Test: It is also known as an alternative of Methylene Blue. In this test, dye contains Haemotoxylin and alum. The body portion is unstained whereas head portion turned to black.

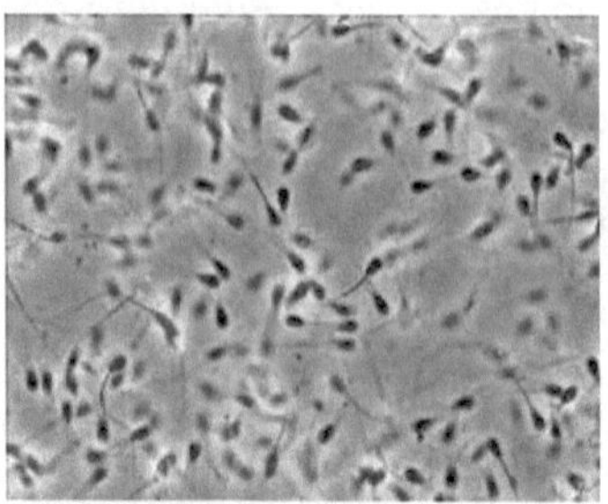

Figure: Hemalum Staining

CASE STUDY:

One famous case that involved semen detection and played a significant role in solving the crime is the case of the Golden State Killer, also known as the East Area Rapist/Original Night Stalker (EAR/ONS). Between 1974 and 1986, the Golden State Killer committed a series of burglaries, rapes, and murders in California. Semen samples were collected from some of the crime scenes, and although DNA profiling techniques were not as advanced at the time, the samples were preserved. Decades later, advancements in forensic DNA analysis allowed investigators to reexamine the evidence. In 2018, using genetic genealogy and comparing DNA from the semen samples to public genealogy databases, authorities identified Joseph James DeAngelo as the Golden State Killer. His DNA matched the samples collected from the crime scenes, leading to his arrest and subsequent conviction in 2020.

2.2 Saliva

Saliva is a watery liquid secreted into the mouth by glands, providing lubrication for chewing and swallowing, and aiding digestion. The human mouth excretes one to two litres of fluid every day. It starts the digestive process in the mouth.

Saliva is a food fluid that mixes with food in the mouth during chewing by teeth. It acts as a digestive juice and softens the food, allowing for an easier digestion process. Salivary glands produce this substance. Moreover, Saliva is a dark, colorless, opalescent fluid found in the mouths of humans and other vertebrates at all times. Air, mucus, proteins, mineral salts, and amylase make up this fluid. Saliva gathers up food waste, bacterial cells, and white blood cells as it circulates in the mouth cavity.

Ph of Saliva: 6.7-7.4

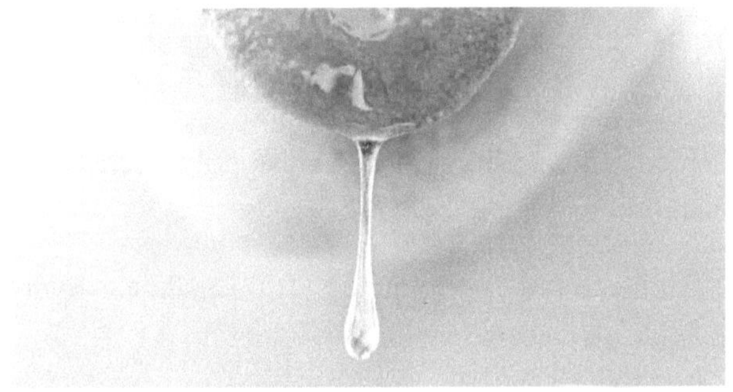

Figure: Human Saliva

Composition of Saliva: In humans, saliva is around 99% water, plus electrolytes, mucus, white blood cells, epithelial cells (from which DNA can be extracted), enzymes (such as lipase and amylase), antimicrobial agents (such as secretory IgA, and lysozymes).

• Water: 99.5%

• Electrolytes:

o 2–21 mmol/L sodium (lower than blood plasma)

o 10–36 mmol/L potassium (higher than plasma)

o 1.2–2.8 mmol/L calcium (similar to plasma)

o 0.08–0.5 mmol/L magnesium o 5–40 mmol/L chloride (lower than plasma)

o 25 mmol/L bicarbonate (higher than plasma)

o 1.4–39 mmol/L phosphate

o Iodine (mmol/L concentration is usually higher than plasma, but dependent variable according to dietary iodine intake)

• Mucus (mucus in saliva of mucopolysaccharides and glycoproteins) mainly consists

• Antibacterial compounds (thiocyanate, hydrogen peroxide, and secretory immunoglobulin A)

• Epidermal growth factor (EGF)

• Saliva eliminates caesium, which can substitute for potassium in the cells.

- Various enzymes; most notably:

o α-amylase (EC3.2.1.1), or ptyalin, secreted by the acinar cells of the parotid and submandibular glands, starts the digestion of starch before the food is even swallowed; it has a pH optimum of 7.4

o Lingual lipase, which is secreted by the acinar cells of the sublingual gland; has a pH optimum around 4.0 so it is not activated until entering the acidic environment of the stomach

o Kallikrein, an enzyme that proteolytically cleaves high molecular-weight kininogen to produce bradykinin, which is a vasodilator; it is secreted by the acinar cells of all three major salivary glands

o Antimicrobial enzymes that kill bacteria:

♣ Lysozyme

♣ Salivary lactoperoxidase

♣ Lactoferrin

♣ Immunoglobulin A

o Proline-rich proteins (function in enamel formation, $Ca2+$ binding, microbe killing and lubrication)

o Minor enzymes including: salivary acid phosphatases A+B, N acetylmuramoyl-L-alanine amidase, NAD(P)H dehydrogenase (quinone), superoxide dismutase, glutathione transferase, class 3 aldehyde dehydrogenase, glucose-6-phosphate isomerase, and tissue kallikrein (function unknown)

- Cells: possibly as many as 8 million human and 500 million bacterial cells per mL. The presence of bacterial products (small organic acids, amines, and thiols) causes saliva to sometimes exhibit a foul odor.

- Opiorphin, a pain-killing substance found in human saliva

- Haptocorrin, a protein which binds to vitamin B12 to protect it against degradation in the stomach, before it binds to intrinsic factor.

Production: The production of saliva is stimulated both by the sympathetic nervous system and the parasympathetic. The saliva stimulated by sympathetic innervation is thicker, and saliva stimulated parasympathetically is more fluid-like. Sympathetic stimulation of saliva is to facilitate respiration, whereas parasympathetic stimulation is to facilitate digestion.

Parasympathetic stimulation leads to acetylcholine (ACh) release onto the salivary acinar cells. ACh binds to muscarinic receptors, specifically M3, and causes an increased intracellular calcium ion concentration (through the IP3/DAG second messenger system). Increased calcium causes vesicles within the cells to fuse with the apical cell membrane leading to secretion. ACh also causes the salivary gland to release kallikrein, an enzyme that converts kininogen to lysyl-bradykinin. Lysyl bradykinin acts upon blood vessels and capillaries of the salivary gland to generate vasodilation and increased capillary permeability, respectively. The resulting increased blood flow to the acini allows the production of more saliva. In addition, Substance P can bind to Tachykinin NK-1 receptors leading to increased intracellular calcium concentrations and subsequently increased saliva secretion. Lastly, both parasympathetic and sympathetic nervous stimulation can lead to myoepithelium contraction which causes the expulsion of secretions from the secretory acinus into the ducts and eventually to the oral cavity. Sympathetic stimulation results in the release of norepinephrine. Norepinephrine binding to α adrenergic receptors will cause an increase in intracellular calcium levels leading to more fluid vs. protein secretion. If norepinephrine binds β-adrenergic receptors, it will result in more protein or enzyme secretion vs. fluid secretion. Stimulation by norepinephrine initially decreases blood flow to the salivary glands due to constriction of blood vessels but this effect is overtaken by vasodilation caused by various local vasodilators.

Saliva as Evidence: In forensics, saliva is used as biological evidence and is very helpful in determining various aspects of an individual such as sex, individuality, ABO blood groups, microbial signature, biomarkers, or habits like smoking.

Saliva shares a great resemblance with plasma as it encompasses similar organic or inorganic compound contents. In forensic casework, identifying any evidence is the primary goal to establish the groundwork for further investigation. It has been widely used as an informative tool in forensic situations like poisoning, hanging, or cases of drug abuse, etc. for more than two decades now.

Saliva may be found in the form of a pool or stained form, but its identification is challenging because of its transparency. The procedure followed in case of Saliva includes its **Location, Collection, Preservation & Packaging,** discussed below.

Location: Keenly observation on following places will locate saliva:

- Saliva is found on clothes, cigarette butt, bottles, cup, Handkerchief, etc. In cases of biting during struggle, assault, kidnapping, Hanging, spitting or tobacco spitting at scene of crime, saliva provides lot of evidentiary data.

Collection: The collection of saliva is a very intricate process that is usually carried out by two swabbing techniques. The choice of technique depends on the type of surface on which evidence gets deposited.

- In a single swab approach, a wet sterile cotton swab which is moistened by distilled water/normal saline is rolled over the collection site. The swabbing is done without applying extra pressure to avoid the collection of the substrate material.

- Though, in double swabbing method, the sample site is swabbed twice. First, a wet cotton swab is rolled over the site, followed by a dry swab. This method ensures maximum collection of saliva from the substrate. The Double swab technique is followed for absorbent surfaces such as skin, cloth, and half-eaten food items, etc. for non-absorbent surfaces, such as plastic evidence, and glasses, etc. the single swab technique is administered.

• While swabbing, the investigator must be careful not to swab beyond the desired site as it could cause unnecessary contamination leading to improper or mixed DNA profiling.

• The double swabbing collection method has been preferred over single swabbing since the former ensures obtaining the maximum amount of evidence from the surface.

Preservation and Packaging: From handling to packaging, chain of custody should be maintained properly.

• To facilitate biochemical and biopharmaceutical studies when cold storage is unavailable, we assessed the stability of saliva samples containing preservatives stored at room temperature over a 1-year period. Two preservative mixtures were evaluated: sodium benzoate and citric acid (P1), and ethyl and propyl paraben (P2).

• After preserving saliva is packed in air tight plastic bag with proper labelling.

After collecting the saliva, the evidence is treated with a series of techniques. These techniques are broadly classified into two—destructive and non-destructive.

The technique which destroys the integrity of evidence after the assessment is known as the destructive technique. In this the evidence treated, cannot be used for further processing or stored for later. Though, integrity of evidence is not affected after assessment in case of non-destructive techniques.

Preliminary Test: The preliminary tests state that saliva "might" be present in the submitted evidence, followed by confirmatory tests. Each test has its advantages and limitations. These tests consume a significant amount of time as well as evidence. The evidence loss in identification analysis cannot be retrieved to its original state unless the test is non-destructive. Due to this, there is very little evidence left to test for DNA profiling to establish the identity. The preliminary tests, also known as presumptive tests, for saliva, are based on the amylase enzyme activity.

Polilight detection

• Polilight is a portable, high-intensity light source used to locate body fluids. This method is the only non-destructive type of presumptive technique for the detection of saliva. It produces an intense narrow band of light with a wavelength between 310 and 650 nm. Forensic light source (FLS) is a common term adapted for any illuminating light source that aids in forensic investigation. It is also known as an Alternating light source (ALS). This method helps in visibility and enhances it for photography. This is rapid and less laborious, particularly for large surfaces.

• Although, saliva is often difficult to locate under Polilight because of the lower fluorescence intensity;

also, the absorbency of the surface acts as a hindrance to fluorescence. There are goggles having certain filters that allow only desirable wavelengths and give peculiar observations. The disadvantage of polilight is that the color of the material hampers the strength of the appearance of the stain also, fluorescence patterns are similar to that of other body fluids, leading to non-specificity.

Phadebas test

• The Phadebas test is a commonly used presumptive assay. Its active component is a blue dye-bound DSM-P, microsphere. The test relies on the alpha-amylase activity of saliva and is prone to multiple pseudo-positive results.

A positive reaction is usually confirmed after the release of blue dye, which results from hydrolyses of starch in the presence of amylase. It gives negative results with animal saliva, fruits, vegetables, and some cleaning solutions other body fluids

• In a recent study, the Phadebas press test has also been reported to detect saliva stains on certain fabrics, and aged stained samples (up to 3 months). Some studies have shown its worth compared to other methods such as Poliligh, starch iodine, and SALIgAE.

On the contrary, the inability of the Phadebas test was also reported to presume the identity of saliva. It depends upon the type of evidence and the surface on which saliva is present.

SALIgAE test

• It is a colorimetric approach to eliminate any possible false-positive reactions given by its counterpart methods- Phadebas and Polilight. Hence, it is a more sensitive approach for preliminary saliva detection. The potency and accuracy of SALIgAE have been studied many times with different approaches. It shows sensitivity, irrelevant to the surface on which the stain is present, like envelopes, soda bottles/cans, and mouth masks, and shows specificity towards human saliva. A positive reaction is the yellow color change of an otherwise colorless solution. However, the reaction time must be confined to 5 min to avoid false positive by other body fluids, which generally takes more than 5 min. On comparative analysis of SALIgAE with other assays, it is found to be better and more sensitive than Phadebas.

• Apart from these benefits, it possesses some disadvantages because of the colorimetric result. For analysis in samples mixed with blood, the significant disadvantage of this colorimetric assay is the generation of false positive reaction. It is also time-consuming, or the procedure involves maximum dilution of the sample beforehand, leading to disadvantages and abuse of evidence.

> In addition, ABO group antigens can also be detected in saliva, if the person is secretor. Approximately 80% individuals are known to be secretors.

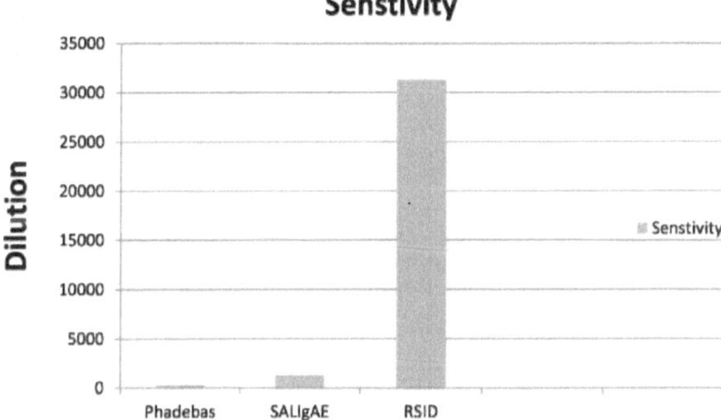

Figure: Sensitivity comparison of Phadebas, SALIgAE, and RSID test

Immunochromatographic strip

A lateral flow immunochromatographic strip works on engaging two monoclonal antibodies present in saliva, making them more sensitive. A common example of this strip is Rapid Stain Identification (RSID) kit. This test is different and much more sensitive than Phadebas or SALIgAE because of its serological approach instead of colorimetric. Many studies have compared these three approaches, and RSID emerged to be much more sensitive and time-effective than its counterparts.

Techniques	Type of technique
Phadebas test	Destructive
SALIgAE test	Destructive
RSID	Destructive
Immunological test	Destructive

RNA profiling	Destructive
DNA methylation	Destructive
UV–Vis Spectroscopy	Destructive

Table: Destructive & non-Destructive Techniques used in Saliva Analysis

Advanced screening/detection techniques: Various detection techniques are considered confirmatory to establish the identity of saliva. Some of these tests have been followed for decades, and some are still emerging.

Immunological techniques

Immunology assays are antigen–antibody-based reactions. These assays not only aid in detection but in species determination as well. Enzyme-linked immunosorbent assay (ELISA) was performed using horseradish peroxidase conjugate combined with monoclonal antibodies to detect the alpha-amylase activity in saliva. This assay has shown no cross-reactivity with either pancreatic or bacterial amylase, but there were still some false positives- 13% of other body fluid. To overcome this, Statherin (STATH), a low molecular weight phosphoprotein secreted by the Parotid gland, was used for detection since it is only present in saliva. The findings gave positive for saliva with no cross-reactivity in ELISA. Also, old-age and mixed saliva samples were readily detected.

Microscopy techniques

Microscopic techniques like SEM (Scanning Electron Microscope) coupled with EDX (Energy Dispersive X-Ray) can identify a specific metal concentration for detection. Some of the trace elements like sodium, phosphorus, sulfur, chlorine, potassium, and calcium are also present in saliva at different concentrations. However, potassium is shown to have the most prominent peak in saliva samples and thus can be used for detection purposes.

RNA profiling

RNA is unstable and prone to degradation, but many studies have shown its stability in samples and its massive use for forensics. The availability of RNAseq by Massively parallel sequencing (MPS) has made the rapid discovery and characterization of novel transcripts and other RNA regions such as non-coding, micro, and small RNA, possible. MicroRNA is a class of small non coding RNA (ncRNA) molecules with 18–24 nucleotides that act as essential regulators for multiple cellular processes and are less susceptible to environmental decay. The degradation rate of RNA in various biological samples over 6 months shows a similar decay pattern that can be analyzed to estimate the sample's age.

Raman spectroscopy

Raman is a widely used and accepted technique in body fluid identification because it provides better spatial resolution and doesn't react with water. Apart from that, Phenylalanine, present amylase and lipase, gives peculiar peaks of saliva in Raman and Thiocyanate, which is found in the saliva of a smoker.

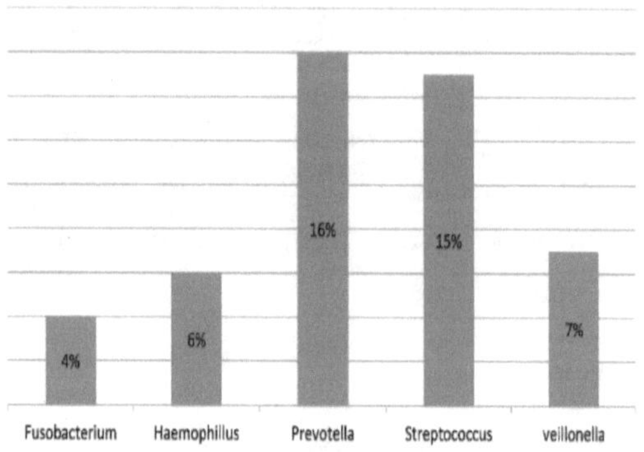

Chart : Microbial Community in Saliva

Microbial detection for saliva identification

Healthy saliva is a mixture of proteins, carbohydrates, antibacterial proteins, white blood cells, and many other components. Though it has antibacterial immunoglobulins and WBCs, forming the first line of defense, it does nurture an array of microbial flora. On average, the total microscopic count is approximately 750 million oral bacteria cells per millilitre of saliva, and of these, streptococci are the most abundant. The presence of these bacteria solely in the saliva has been studied over the years by various techniques such as PCR and loop-mediated isothermal amplification. Over the years, the interest in microbiome identification of body fluids has increased drastically among forensic scientists. There have been multiple studies that show definite positive detection but are performed differently.

CASE STUDY:

One famous case that involved saliva as forensic evidence is the case of Richard Ramirez, also known as the Night Stalker. Ramirez was a notorious serial killer and rapist who terrorized the Los Angeles area in the 1980s. During his crime spree, Ramirez left behind saliva on multiple crime scenes, including bite marks on his victims. Forensic investigators were able to collect and analyze the saliva samples, extracting DNA from the saliva left at the scenes. Years later, in 2009, the DNA evidence obtained from the saliva was matched to Richard Ramirez through a DNA database. The saliva samples conclusively linked him to the crimes, leading to his arrest and subsequent conviction. The use of saliva as forensic evidence played a pivotal role in identifying and bringing Richard Ramirez to justice, providing crucial DNA evidence that connected him to the crime scenes and the victims. The case serves as an example of how saliva analysis can be instrumental in solving high-profile criminal case.

2.3 Sweat

Sweat is a fluid secreted by the sweat glands also called sudoriferous glands. The process of production of sweat is called sweating or perspiration. Sweat glands are the exocrine glands which secretes their production onto epithelial cells by the specific ducts.

pH 4.5 -7.0

There are two types of sweat glands:

- Apocrine glands – they are mostly present at the armpit area, and genital areas.
- Eccrine glands – these glands cover the major surface area of the body. They are present most in the soles and palms then, the head and least in the trunk region.

Eccrine or merocrine gland	**Apocrine gland**
Secretes sweat directly onto the surface of the skin.	Secrete fluid into the sac of hair follicle through which it eventually comes out on the skin.
Simple, coiled, tubular glands	Branched glands
All over the body	Few in numbers

Table: Difference between Eccrine and Apocrine Gland

Osmidrosis: Often called **bromhidrosis,** especially in combination with hyperhidrosis. Osmohidrosis is excessive odor from apocrine sweat glands (which are overactive in the axillae). Osmidrosis is thought to be caused by changes in the apocrine gland structure rather than changes in the bacteria that acts on sweat.

Structure of Sweat gland- Sweat glands comprise a secretory unit and a duct through which sweat or secretory product is passed. Sweat glands are situated in the dermis and are surrounded by adipose tissue. At the base of each sweat gland there is a structure known as the secretory coil. This is surrounded by contractile myoepithelial cells which act to help secrete the gland's product. The contraction of these cells are either controlled by hormones or nerve action.

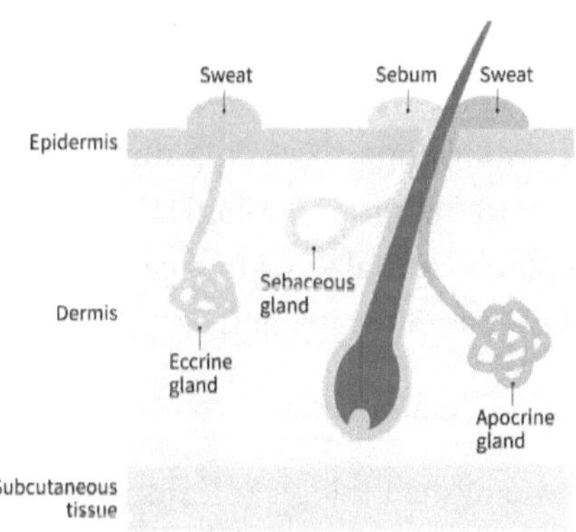

Figure: Structure of Sweat Gland

Composition of Sweat: Majorly water & tracc amounts of lactic acid, minerals, urea. Minerals are-

- Sodium (0.9 gram/litre)

- Potassium (0.2 g/ litre)
- Calcium (0.015 g/ litre)
- Magnesium (0.0013 g/ litre)
- Zinc (0.4 milligrams/litre)
- Copper (0.3–0.8 mg/ litre)
- Iron (1 mg/ litre)
- Chromium (0.1 mg/ litre)
- Nickel (0.05 mg/ litre)
- Lead (0.05 mg/ litre)

Sweat as Evidence

An average square inch of skin contains 650 sweat glands. That means our bodies leave small amounts of sweat on everything we touch — whether we're making a phone call, eating supper or committing a crime. Sweat stains become an important biological evidence in cases like kidnapping, sexual assault etc. Sweat can be analysed for determining ethanol, drugs, ions and metals.

Examination of Sweat includes:

1. **Sweat** is one of the biological fluid which exhibits the blood group substances if the person is a secretor, therefore, the analysis of blood group can be done by examination of sweat. Sweat from secretor individual will contain the Antigens A, B, and H.

2. **Odour** – A small bit from the suspected sample is taken and heated. The specific odour that comes out is taken note of.3.

3. **Gee's urea nitrate test** – The sweat bearing areas are first examined for the presence of urea by the Gee's urea nitrate test. If the positive result is found then it is subjected to absorption inhibition, absorption elution or mixed agglutination test for the identification of blood grouping antigens in them. The crystals appear will have following characteristics: long, colourless, rhombic shaped.

Figure: Crystals from Gee's Test

SEM coupled with EDX – It can identify the relative concentrations of sodium, phosphorus, sulfur, chlorine, potassium, calcium, and other metal traces. The sweat analysis showed that chlorine and sodium were the only consistently clear peaks among the different samples, and potassium was sometimes visible. The large chlorine peak is used as the basis of comparison and identification.

CASE STUDY:

One famous case that was solved using sweat evidence is the case of Ronald Cotton, a wrongful conviction for rape in 1984. Jennifer Thompson, the victim, positively identified Cotton as her attacker based on her memory and a lineup identification. However, years later, DNA testing became available and revealed that Cotton was innocent. During the investigation, sweat stains were found on the victim's clothing. Advances in DNA testing allowed forensic experts to extract DNA from the sweat evidence. When the DNA was compared to Ronald Cotton's DNA, it did not match. The DNA evidence from the sweat stains ultimately led to the exoneration of Ronald Cotton and the identification of the true perpetrator, Bobby Poole. This case highlights the importance of sweat evidence and DNA testing in correcting wrongful convictions and ensuring justice is served.

www.ingramcontent.com/pod-product-compliance
Lightning Source LLC
LaVergne TN
LVHW041132150826
845673LV00007B/2285

* 9 7 9 8 8 9 7 2 4 6 7 5 5 *